THE NET WILL APPEAR

Erin Mallon

I0139930

BROADWAY PLAY PUBLISHING INC
New York
www.broadwayplaypublishing.com
info@broadwayplaypublishing.com

Cover photo by Craig Wallace Dale

First edition: December 2023
I S B N: 978-0-88145-996-8

Book design: Marie Donovan
Page make-up: Adobe InDesign
Typeface: Palatino

NOTE ON MUSIC

For performance of copyrighted songs, arrangements or recordings referenced in this play, permission of the copyright owner(s) must be obtained. Other songs, arrangements or recordings may be substituted provided permission from the copyright owner(s) of such songs, arrangements or recordings is obtained, or songs, arrangements or recordings in the public domain may be substituted.

THE NET WILL APPEAR had its World Premiere at Mile Square Theater (Artistic Director Chris O'Connor) in Hoboken, NJ in September 2017. The cast and creative contributors were:

BERNARD .... Richard Masur
RORY .... Matilda Lawler

Director ....Mark Cirnigliaro
Set .... Matthew J Fick
Lights ....Justin A Partier & Jenn Burkhardt
Original music & sound ....Sean Hagerty
Costumes..Peter Fogel
Production stage management.......................Jack Cummins

THE NET WILL APPEAR had its Off-Broadway premiere co-produced by Mile Square Theater and The Collective NY at 59E59 Theaters (Artistic Director Val Day) in New York City in December 2018.The cast and creative contributors were:

BERNARD .... Richard Masur
RORY ....Eve Johnson

Director..Mark Cirnigliaro
Set .... Matthew J Fick
Lights .... Justin A Partier & Jenn Burkhardt
Original music & sound ....Sean Hagerty
Costumes...Peter Fogel
Production stage management.......................Jack Cummins
Assistant stage management .... Annette Hammond
Casting... Judy Bowman

CHARACTERS & SETTING

BERNARD, *75 years old*
RORY, *9 years old*

Scene: The rooftops of two houses built quite close together.
Time: The span of one year.

Part One

(The rooftops of two houses built very close together.)

(A man [BERNARD] sits on his roof in a folding beach chair with convenient cup holder. He reads the newspaper and takes sips from the beverage beside him. There is a small cooler by his feet. He's been here a while. He closes his eyes and takes in the sun.)

(Suddenly, the chirpy sounds of a small bird. He immediately gets out of his chair.)

BERNARD: Hooowah! *(Note: that's the struggle sound he makes when hoisting himself out of chairs.)*

(BERNARD tiptoes toward the tree, which houses the bird. He watches intently. The chirping continues.)

BERNARD: Come on. Come on you little cretin. Just a few more inches. Yep, hop hop hop you feathery little—

(The bird flies away.)

BERNARD: Yeah, you better fly away! I don't wanna see your bird ass back here, you hear me? You're a loser, bird! A loser!

(BERNARD returns to his chair, takes a gulp of his drink and continues reading. A red laser point shines on his newspaper. He lowers the paper and the red light beams directly into his forehead.)

BERNARD: Jesus!

(BERNARD *darts out of the way. The laser point seems to follow him. He sends his voice toward his window.*)

BERNARD: Honey??? Honey….!?

(*No matter which way* BERNARD *turns the laser finds him. It's going berserk now, scribbling every which way over his chest. He's on the verge of hyperventilating.*)

BERNARD: (*To himself*) You're imagining it. You're imagining it. (*He makes the sign of the cross and closes his eyes, waiting.*) Shit! What are you—?

(*The laser disappears. The window on the house next door has opened. A young girl [*RORY*] pops her head out.*)

RORY: Were you praying? Cool! I pray now too! Which one you doin'? Hail Mary? Our Father? Act of Contrition?

BERNARD: What's that in your hand?

RORY: A laser pointer.

(*Beat*)

BERNARD: You shouldn't point lasers at people.

RORY: Why not?

BERNARD: Because they might think they're being—

RORY: I wasn't pointing it at you on purpose though, I was using it for my cat, Dr. Phil. His cat pop-tomotrist said I'm supposed to stimulate him as much as possible 'cause he's going blind from this thing called lens luxation? It's where he feels like he's always looking through a long tube. Watch. (*She disappears and shouts from inside her house.*) CAN YOU SEE HIM FROM THERE? HE GOES CRAZY FOR THIS THING!

BERNARD: That there is animal abuse.

(RORY *pops her head back out.*)

RORY: What?

BERNARD: You're abusing that animal.

RORY: Nuh-uh! I love Dr Phil!

BERNARD: I'm sure you do but consider this… Cats are tactile creatures. When they pounce on their prey they rely on being able to feel their captured treasure underneath their paws. Imagine doing a great job of stalking and pouncing and repeatedly NEVER feeling as if you've successfully captured your intended target.

RORY: Huh?

BERNARD: Your "cat pop-tomotrist" is an idiot.

RORY: Okay. *(She hops out onto her roof.)*

BERNARD: Easy kid, easy.

RORY: Your name's Great Dane, right?

(Beat)

BERNARD: No. Bernard.

RORY: Oh! Right right. I knew it was the name of some huge awesome dog. We got your mail once. Rory Landis. Fourth grader. I'm going to be a choreographer, a dolphin trainer and a detective when I grow up.

BERNARD: You're gonna be all three?

RORY: Yes, I will excel equally at all three.

BERNARD: Good luck with that.

RORY: Thanks!

BERNARD: I suppose if a dancing dolphin goes missing—

RORY: I'll be the one to call, that's exactly right, friend. So how was your Passover?

BERNARD: I'm Episcopalian.

RORY: You shouldn't call yourself an alien. "Undocumented worker" is nicer. Anyway, my Passover sucked.

BERNARD: You're Jewish?

RORY: Yup.

BERNARD: So why are you wearing a Catholic school uniform?

RORY: "It's the best place for me right now."

BERNARD: A Catholic school.

RORY: Yup.

BERNARD: How's that working out?

RORY: Not so well actually! This Jesus guy is really throwing me for a loop. Every time I ask a question about him, I get sent to the principal's office. I was there three times today. So anyway, this was my first year not searching for the afikomen. I ALWAYS search for the afikomen at Passover dinner. But this year it was "Pearl's turn to do it" 'cause "she's the youngest now." Such a joke. She didn't even search! My mom just like stuck her places, propped up by pillows and said "Where is it, Pearl? Where's the afikomen?" And she just looked around like this. *(She makes Pearl's dopey baby face.)* And everyone clapped! So stupid. Hey, how come we've never talked before?

BERNARD: Boy, I just don't know.

RORY: Me neither. We've been living here almost a whole month.

BERNARD: You don't say! I barely noticed twenty-five and a half days of non-stop dog barkin' and newborn wailing.

RORY: Oh good! My mom thought we might be bothering you. Does your face hurt?

BERNARD: No. Why.

RORY: 'Cause you hold it like this. *(She scowls.)*

RORY: Like your face hurts.

BERNARD: No I don't. *(He's scowling exactly like she is.)*

RORY: Okay. So why are you hanging out on your roof? I've never seen you out here before. Once I saw you at the deli yelling at the cashier lady. You were so—

BERNARD: Shh shh shh.

RORY: What?

BERNARD: Look!

RORY: Where?!

(BERNARD points.)

BERNARD: There!

RORY: There where?! Where am I looking?!

BERNARD: There!

RORY: WHERE??!

BERNARD: Do you not know how pointing works, kid? Follow my damn finger!

RORY: Oh.

(Beat. BERNARD and RORY look down at her lawn.)

BERNARD: First robin sighting of the season. Look at that beautiful red breast.

RORY: You said breast.

BERNARD: I did.

RORY: So now do I get to say something dirty too?

BERNARD: No.

RORY: Balls.

BERNARD: Stop that!

RORY: What? You got to!

BERNARD: There is nothing dirty about the word breast in the context of—or even in the context of a woman's—will you just look at the damn bird?

RORY: Sure!

(BERNARD *and* RORY *watch the bird.*)

RORY: You say damn a lot.

BERNARD: Fuck yeah I do.

(Beat)

RORY: This is a nice moment, us looking at this breasty bird together. Before you get too attached to me though, I should tell you something.

BERNARD: What's that.

RORY: I'm going to jail soon.

BERNARD: That so?

RORY: Super so.

BERNARD: Interesting. What'd you do?

RORY: Took the tag off my new pillow.

BERNARD: Okay…

RORY: Which is a crazy illegal thing to do! Says so right on the tag: "Made in China. Under PENALTY OF LAW this tag not to be removed except by THE CONSUMER." The other day I saw a Chinese man at Tar-jhay and I almost threw up. What if he is "THE CONSUMER"? What if he was sent here to Toledo to consume me and arrest me?

BERNARD: Actually, "The Consumer" is— *(Quick beat)* Wow, you're up shit's crick, kid! What'd you do with the evidence?

RORY: The tag? Got rid of it. Buried it in the backyard.

BERNARD: Smart move!

RORY: I thought so!

BERNARD: Well, we'll have to look out for each other, because…I also am a pellow criminal.

RORY: You've cut off tags too?!!?

BERNARD: Of course not, I'm not an animal! Listen—

RORY: Did you machine wash them when you're only supposed to spot treat!??

BERNARD: LISTEN. My wife Irma and I used to love going to hotels. Made us feel…luxurious. Sometimes we'd go to the Ramada Inn right down the road, just to be wild ya know?

RORY: No, I don't know! Wild how!?

BERNARD: We'd have a…a special adult night.

RORY: Like you grabbed a ton of wine coolers and locked yourself in the bedroom where you played R rated movies really loud so no one else could hear what was going on inside?

(Beat)

BERNARD: Sure, yeah. Anyway, Irma was always real frugal. And smart. So smart. So, each time we'd go, we'd bring our own shitty pellows in our own shitty pellow cases and then…we'd swap 'em out for the Ramada's fluffy new ones. Did that for over forty years. Never bought a pellow in my life.

RORY: Whoa! The Consumer is going to "beat BOTH our asses!" Also, you say pillow weird.

BERNARD: What. Pellow.

RORY: Pillow.

BERNARD: Pellow.

RORY: Pillow

BERNARD: Pellow.

RORY: Pillow.

BERNARD: That's what I said! PELLOW!!!

(Beat)

RORY: I like you. Can I call you Bern?

BERNARD: No.

RORY: How about Nard?

BERNARD: No.

RORY: Tor-nardo?

BERNARD: Absolutely not.

RORY: You're right, Nard's better.

(Suddenly, the sound of a barking dog, if it can be called barking. It's a truly heinous sound.)

RORY: That's Joy Behar, our dalmatian. She's pure bred.

BERNARD: Of course she is.

RORY: Did you know dalmatians are depicted in cave paintings riding behind chariots?

BERNARD: I did not know that.

RORY: Did you know that they're born white and gain their spots as they mature and that they have spots in their mouths and even on their buttholes?

BERNARD: Alright then.

RORY: You're not impressed by those facts?

BERNARD: I'm more of a mutt man, myself.

RORY: Oh. Mutts are dirty.

(The ungodly sound continues.)

BERNARD: Is there a reason your dog sounds like a tortured hyena?

RORY: Dalmatians are prone to deafness and bladder stones. We're pretty sure Joy Behar's passing one right now. Don't worry, my mom will call her back inside soon.

BERNARD: Doesn't your mom mind you being up there on that roof? Not exactly safe, you know.

RORY: My mother needs me to "stay out of her hair" for "just one day, Rory! GO UPSTAIRS!!!!!" *(Quick beat)* Technically I am "upstairs".

(The dog sounds stop.)

RORY: Oh see? She's going in. *(She starts pummeling the fronts of her legs.)* Arrrr, slappyslappyslappyslappyslappyslappy.

BERNARD: What in the hell are you doin'?

RORY: I think I'm growth spurting. My shin meat hurts.

BERNARD: Your shin "meat"?

RORY: Yeah, "we're all made of meat, wouldn't you say? Meatsuits walking the world, our true essences hidden under all the gristle?"

BERNARD: Who are you regurgitating?

RORY: Regurgiwhat?

BERNARD: You're spitting out someone else's words.

RORY: Ya know, once my grandma told me "you're the spit from your father's mouth." I wanted to kick her.

BERNARD: So why didn't you?

RORY: 'Cause she's my grandma.

BERNARD: Okay.

RORY: Plus, she didn't mean to be gross, she just meant I look like him.

BERNARD: You don't look a thing like that douche.

RORY: Yes I do, I look exactly like that douche! Wait, what's a douche?

BERNARD: A douche is someone who parks his Lexus Hybrid in front of other people's houses, bathes in buckets of Vidal Sassoon hair gel, and sculpts his lawn in suburban Ohio to look like the Gardens of Versailles. THAT'S a douche.

RORY: Oh, you're talking about Bob. Bob isn't my dad-dad, he's my bonus-dad. He's Pearl's dad-dad though.

BERNARD: Oh, he's your stepdad.

RORY: No. People don't say "step" anymore. They say "bonus." I get a "bonus dad."

BERNARD: Spare me. Where's your real dad?

RORY: Sin-sin-atty. There's lots of sin there. So what's your house like inside? Bet there's lots of wood paneling and sad wallpaper in there, huh?

BERNARD: Excuse me?

RORY: Your house is "a study in decay."

BERNARD: What the hell are you talking about?

RORY: "Lonely old people never renovate their houses. They let their curb appeal go to shit and bring down the quality of the neighborhood for the rest of us."

BERNARD: I'm going inside. *(He stands.)* Hoowah!

RORY: No, don't go! *(She stands.)* Hoowah!

BERNARD: What are you—?

RORY: I bet your wallpaper is really nice! And I think your curb is totally appealing!

BERNARD: I'm not lonely. I wake up next to my best friend every morning of my life.

RORY: How come your best friend doesn't sleep in his own bed?

BERNARD: No, my wife. I wake up next to my wife. She's my best friend.

RORY: Oh! Cool! I thought she was dead! I thought you had a dead wife!

(Beat)

BERNARD: Why the hell would you think that?

RORY: I guess 'cause nobody ever sees her?

BERNARD: I never see Beyonce. Is Beyonce dead?

RORY: No. Beyonce will never die. *(Beat)* Also, you talk about her in the past tense.

(Beat)

BERNARD: My wife is inside. She just doesn't want to see me right now.

RORY: You got in a fight? That's ok, "Divorce is sometimes the best thing for the family."

BERNARD: I will never divorce Irma! Never!

RORY: Okay!

(Silence)

RORY: So a Beyonce fan, huh?

(BERNARD pours himself more to drink and gulps it down.)

RORY: My parakeet's name is Ja Rule. I just made him a ladder out of popsicle sticks to help him strengthen his bum leg.

BERNARD: What's with all the animal invalids?

RORY: Huh?

BERNARD: Sounds like you're runnin' a veterinary hospital over there.

RORY: Oh they're not all sick. We have a super healthy hamster named Jimmy Fallon. For a second we thought he had hamster cancer 'cause one morning we noticed these big bumps on his belly? But turns out those were just his testicles descending. So that was awesome news. But yeah, there's lots to take care of over here. My mom's always like "IF I HAVE TO CLEAN UP ONE MORE CREATURE'S POOP I'M GONNA...!" Oh hey, speaking of poop...

BERNARD: Let's not.

RORY: ...according to family legend, when I was learning how to use the shitter— My dad always called it "the shitter" —I used to cry every time we flushed my poop. Apparently it made me really sad to flush a part of myself down the tubes. Scared me or something. Anyway, I'm over that now. I almost never cry anymore when I do number two. Hey, did you know babies poop black? Pearl pooped a whole diaper full of sticky black her first day home.

(BERNARD *refills his glass again and shoots it back.*)

RORY: Tasty drink, huh? Wow, those are interesting decorations.

BERNARD: What? Where?

RORY: In your tree. Are those mouse traps in your tree?

BERNARD: ...Yes.

RORY: How come? You have mice in your tree?

BERNARD: Sparrows.

RORY: YOU'RE KILLING SPARROWS???

BERNARD: Not yet.

RORY: WITH MOUSETRAPS???

BERNARD: I haven't actually caught any yet, but—

RORY: WHY ARE YOU KILLING SPARROWS WITH MOUSETRAPS???! Oh God!!! (*She bursts into tears.*)

BERNARD: Jesus Christ...

RORY: JESUS CHRIST HATES YOU FOR THIS!! Birds??? Stay away from this place! This place is "cloaked in hellfire"!

BERNARD: Geez, What?! I'll take them down. Just stop crying.

RORY: You'll take 'em down?

BERNARD: I will. I'll… I'll take them down.

RORY: Okay. *(She quiets.)*

(Beat)

BERNARD: You done crying?

RORY: Yeah, I'm done. *(Beat)* I have to pee now though. I'm an emotional pee-er.

BERNARD: Alright. You go take care of that. Nice meeting you.

RORY: Oh, I'll be back, Nard.

BERNARD: Can't wait.

(RORY crawls through the window into her house.)

BERNARD: *(To himself)* Shit.

(RORY immediately pops her head back out the window.)

RORY: "Mousetraps in the trees." If I ever write a horror movie about you, that's what it will be called.

BERNARD: Go on kid, go!

(RORY goes inside. BERNARD sits back in his chair and reaches for his drink.)

(BERNARD stares at his window. He gets out of his chair.)

BERNARD: Hoowah! *(He taps on his window with his wedding ring.)* Sweetheart? *(Beat)* Sweetheart, I know you can hear me. *(Beat)* I just saw a robin. You used to get so excited when you saw your first robin of the season. Remember that? Maybe she'll come back. You want to come to the window and have a look? *(Beat)* Irms…I know you've had a really hard morning. I just wanted to touch you. To comfort you. I love you sweetheart, I—

RORY: So!

BERNARD: *(Startled)* Geezuz!

(RORY climbs back onto her roof.)

RORY: I gave "sparrows" a google. Some reeeeeeally interesting findings.

BERNARD: I thought you were peeing.

RORY: False alarm. So, listen. They're really smart and have all these feelings. They sing louder when there's traffic 'cause they wanna be heard. They also sing louder when there's been infidelity in the nest.

BERNARD: Do you even know what infidelity is?

RORY: Yup, it's... *(She juts her head in her window to read off her computer screen.)* "A violation of a couple's assumed or stated contract regarding emotional and/ or sexual exclusivity."

(RORY's butt is in the air, her skirt every which way. BERNARD shields his eyes.)

BERNARD: Kid, could you just—

(RORY pops back out.)

RORY: So maybe your sparrow is super loud and sad because her contract was violated. And you're totally gonna make her day worse when you snap her in your trapper. Don't snap her in your trapper. Beat. Wait. You like robins?

BERNARD: Of course. Robins are beautiful harbingers of Spring.

RORY: But sparrows...?

BERNARD: Satanic little shits that wake me up every morning.

RORY: You're a bird racist. You need to work on that, friend. Hey, do you have kids?

BERNARD: No.

RORY: Wow! So hanging out with me today must be so much fun for you!

BERNARD: Fantastic, yes.

RORY: I have a wart in my pocket. Wanna see?

BERNARD: You have a what?

RORY: A wart. In my pocket. (*Pinches something very tiny between her fingers and holds it up. Showing the heel of her hand*) It used to live here, but I sliced it off on accident. Monkey bars are nuts. Anyway, it's super cool so I couldn't throw it out. (*Beat*) I dropped it. Ohmygod I dropped it! (*Whining sound*)

BERNARD: Not to worry, I'm sure some other fascinating fungus will sprout on your body soon enough.

RORY: Ohmygod, I hope so! It was like the tiniest English muffin you've ever seen! All these neat nooks and crannies.

BERNARD: You're gonna love getting old, kid.

RORY: Yeah?

BERNARD: My feet are like two boat bottoms. Barnacles for days.

RORY: Amazing! Ooooh can you show me?

(BERNARD *does not show* RORY.)

RORY: So. I'm starting a new club. Wanna be in it?

BERNARD: Not at all.

RORY: Aw! Join it, join it, join my club.

BERNARD: Not much of a joiner.

RORY: But this club is totally "up your alley"!

BERNARD: What the hell do you know about my "alley"?

RORY: Come on, friend, be in my club!

BERNARD: Now, why do you do that?

RORY: What.

BERNARD: Call me "friend?"

RORY: Aren't you? Aren't you my friend?

(Beat)

BERNARD: Oh hell. Why not.

(Beat)

*(*RORY *looks like she may explode from happiness.)*

RORY: I'M GONNA DANCE FOR YOU!!! I have a recital coming up and I'm real nervous about it so I'm gonna tap dance for you!

BERNARD: Please don't.

RORY: Great. I'll go get my shoes.

*(*BERNARD *goes back to his window. He taps on it again.)*

BERNARD: Honey? *(Taps)* Sweetheart? *(Taps again)* I wish you'd just— Alright, well, if you need me, I'm right outside ok? Happy to come in whenever you feel comfortable. Just say the word and I— *(Beat)* Hi beautiful. *(Beat)* Thank you for— How're you feeling now? *(Beat)* Is there anything I can—

RORY: I'M BACK!

BERNARD: Christ, kid!

RORY: Who were you talking to?

BERNARD: Oh god, she's in costume.

*(*RORY *emerges in a glittery unitard and starts setting up her portable speakers.)*

RORY: Sort of. There's a headpiece thingy which my mom still needs to hot glue the feathers on. And there's spats for my taps that still need rhinestones, but you can use your imagination for those, yeah?

*(*BERNARD *looks torn between the window and* RORY. *She presses play on her iPod. Something like Elton John's*

Crocodile Rock *plays. She begins her routine and shouts over the music.)*

RORY: Are you familiar wity Sir Elton John? He's married to a boy, did you know that?!

BERNARD: Listen kid, I—

RORY: Shuffle step! Shuffle step!
Shuffle HOP step, shuffle step!
Heel spank step! Heel spank step!
Toe-toe-heel-heel, Toe-toe-heel-heel!
Heel spank step!
(She continues the routine.)

RORY: What do you think? Do I have talent?

BERNARD: Eh.

RORY: Thank you! I've been told I have a wedgie problem!

BERNARD: You have a what?

RORY: I pick my costume wedgies while I'm onstage and I don't even know I'm doing it! So watch me real close, and if you see me reaching for my wedge I need you to scream real loud at me like someone's dying okay?

BERNARD: I'm not going to do that

RORY: Like someone's dying!

BERNARD: No.

RORY: Come on, you need to!

BERNARD: Don't tell me what I need to—

RORY: But you need to!

BERNARD: No I do not.

RORY: Please you neeeeed to!

BERNARD: AHHHHHHHHHHHH!

(RORY *turns off the music.*)

(*Silence*)

RORY: Why'd you yell, Nard? My hand wasn't anywhere near my butt.

BERNARD: Stop with the Nard stuff. (*He's packing up his things.*)

RORY: Wait, where are you going?

BERNARD: I just—I can't— (*Beat*) Let's give Bernard a little break, huh? I need a break.

RORY: Totally, we need a break from all the dancing. We could memorize the lyrics to some Billie Eilish songs if you want?

BERNARD: No.

RORY: Make paper bag puppets and put on a show?

BERNARD: No.

RORY: Pedicures?

BERNARD: I need a break from YOU, kid.

(*Beat*)

RORY: Oh. Okay.

BERNARD: Sorry, I… (*Beat*) Sorry. (*He disappears inside his house.*)

(RORY *is left alone on her roof.*)

Part Two

(RORY *stands on her roof, one eye glued to a telescope pointed directly at* BERNARD's *window. A beach lounge chair is placed beside her. She sings:*)

RORY: He rocks in the tree tops all day long
Hoppin' and a-boppin' and a-singing his song

(BERNARD *appears in the window.*)

BERNARD: Hey kid.

(*Blood curdling scream by* RORY. *She throws the telescope down, hurls herself into the lounge chair, lifts a piece of cardboard wrapped in aluminum foil under her chin and closes her eyes.*)

(BERNARD *gets on his roof and places his drink on the windowsill.*)

(*Silence*)

BERNARD: Catchin' some rays, huh? A good day for that. (*Beat*) How've ya been? (*Beat*) Not talking to me, huh?

RORY: If you'll excuse me a moment. (*Shouting to street*) Hola Paolo! Muchas Gracias para tu ayudar con nuestros arboles de naranjas. I mean…manzanas, yeah manzanas. Mi… "padre de bonus" …es muy feliz con tu trabajar. When you're done, tu dinero es a lado de la…can de trash? Basura basura! Comprendes? Ah comprendes! (*She gives Paolo a thumbs up, then giggles uncontrollably. She recovers. To* BERNARD) Our gardener, Paolo. (*She returns to her tanning and resumes "ignoring" Bernard.*)

BERNARD: Practicing some Spanish?

RORY: Bob enrolled me in a language immersion day camp. I'm trilingual now.

BERNARD: Wow.

RORY: Yeah, a lot can happen in three months.

BERNARD: English, Spanish…what's your third language?

RORY: British.

BERNARD: Hm.

RORY: I've picked that up on my own though. *(Donning a British accent)* It's quite similar to English, but you use this voice and say things like al-yoo-MIN-yum and WANK-uh.

BERNARD: Well, good for you. *(Beat)* See anything good?

RORY: Where?

BERNARD: Through my window, see anything interesting?

RORY: I don't know what you're talking about.

BERNARD: Telescope.

RORY: What's a telescope?

BERNARD: Alright. Well hey, maybe you can help me with this. We seem to have a little raccoon who's started rummaging around in our trash. In broad daylight. Wearing sparkly sneakers. Know anything about her?

(Beat)

RORY: That's classified. Club stuff.

BERNARD: People have a right to their privacy. If someone wants to share information with you, they will. The snooping you've been doin', the… telescoping…it's rude. Cut it out.

RORY: I'm not rude, I'm resourceful! I started a one-man dumpster diving detective agency!

BERNARD: A "one man" operation, huh?

RORY: Well yeah, you didn't want to be involved. Bet you're regretting that now that I'm giving you the cold shoulder, huh?

BERNARD: Is that what this is?

RORY: Yup, I'm a "frigid bitch."

BERNARD: Whoa! Where'd you learn that term?

RORY: Dunno. My house is our headquarters, AKA "The Ror-shack". Get it? 'Cause I'm Rory and this is my shack?

BERNARD: Clever.

RORY: Thanks. I've learned so much about our neighbors through my new endeavor. Mrs Cabe is a Listerine-aholic, that new family with the Pitbull eats a TON of Cinnamon Toast Crunch and you know Mr Connolly with the weird mailbox? He buys head lice shampoo on a regular basis. Hey, I've rung your doorbell a whole lot the past few weeks but you never answer. I know you're in there. I can hear Judge Judy.

(BERNARD *ignores* RORY *and takes a swig of his drink.*)

RORY: What is that that orangey stuff you're always drinking?

(*Beat*)

BERNARD: Juice.

RORY: I love juice, I'm a juice-aholic!

BERNARD: Don't do that.

RORY: What.

BERNARD: Add -aholic to things. That's not nice.

RORY: Why? It means you really like something. I'm also a dance-aholic, a Chapstick-aholic and a mac-n-cheese-aholic. Is it Jim Beam juice? (*Beat*) The bottles in your recycling bin all say Jim Beam on them.

BERNARD: Yes, it's...Jim Beam juice.

RORY: Can I have a sip?

BERNARD: No, it's an adult beverage. Besides, what am I gonna do, throw it at you?

RORY: Good point. You know what we need? A conveyor belt. If we had a conveyor belt connecting our roofs we could share toys and adult beverages all day long. I'll make us one.

BERNARD: How are you going to do that?

RORY: Bob enrolled me in a Saturday morning Lego robotics class.

BERNARD: How many things does Bob have you enrolled in?

RORY: "As many as it takes."

BERNARD: Isn't robotics for boys?

RORY: (Gasp) You're sexy!

BERNARD: I think you mean sexist.

RORY: You're sexist! You need to work on that.

BERNARD: Whatever happened to playing with barbies?

RORY: "Barbie's beauty ideal is unhealthy and damaging."

BERNARD: Whoa. My daughter played with barbies. And anyway, didn't I just read that they have Fat Barbie now?

RORY: Ew. Who wants a fat Barbie? Hey, you said you didn't have kids! What's her name?

(Beat)

BERNARD: Chrissy.

RORY: Did people call her Pissy Chrissy at recess?

BERNARD: Not that I'm aware of.

RORY: 'Cause that would be the obvious choice if I wanted to make fun of her.

BERNARD: Why would you want to do that?

RORY: I wouldn't, but lots of people would. As soon as kids learn your name they're figuring out how to rhyme you straight into hell, so you have to be prepared. I'm "Rory, Rory, she's so whorey, so butt-ugly you need a suppository."

BERNARD: Christ, that's vulgar. And strangely sophisticated. Well, there's not much they could do with Bernard.

RORY: Are you kidding me? *(Beat)*
Bernard Bernard, such a tard
He's got a big round belly and cooks with lard
His veiny, purple legs look like swiss chard
Bernard, Bernard, He has a messy yard
He's got wrinkles on his face and his arms are scarred
He has a six thousand dollar balance on his AMEX card—

BERNARD: Alright, alright.

RORY: I could keep going.

BERNARD: No thank you.

RORY: See what I mean? That stuff can hurt your feelings. That's why I'm going to protect my daughter and name her Ruh-JAI-nuh. There's absolutely no way you can make fun of a name as gorgeous as Ruh-JAI-nuh.

BERNARD: I believe it's pronounced Ruh-JEAN-uh.

RORY: Ew. *(Beat)* I shouldn't have said the word tard. I felt bad as soon as it came out. My rhymer wasn't warmed up yet. You got any pictures of her?

BERNARD: Of Chrissy?

RORY: Yeah.

BERNARD: 'Course I do. You wanna see?

RORY: Hold on, hold on. *(She waves at someone at street level.)* Hi Chuck! Don't worry, Joy Behar is in the sunroom, so she can't do that thing to your leg again. You got any packages for me? No??? 'Cause I'm waiting for a pretty intense Lego delivery. Alright, well stay cool, man. Bye! *(Beat)* That was Chuck, our mailman.

BERNARD: I know. He's my mailman too.

RORY: Whoa! What are the odds? Isn't Chuck a terrible name? I feel so bad for him. I made a real push to rename him Charles, but I guess he doesn't know that he deserves love. *(She looks toward* BERNARD's *tree.)* So you lied to me, huh?

(Beat)

BERNARD: What? No I did not. What about?

RORY: Mousetraps are still up.

BERNARD: Oh.

RORY: It's okay. Grown-ups lie all the time.

(Silence)

(BERNARD *looks back at his window.)*

BERNARD: Alright, I've been out here too— *(Quick beat)* I'm headed inside. *(He gets up.)* Hoowah!

(RORY *gets up.)*

RORY: Hoowah!

BERNARD: Why do you do that?

RORY: What. Hoowah?

BERNARD: Yes.

RORY: So I can be like you.

BERNARD: I do that?

RORY: All the time. I like it! Makes standing up feel special. *(She sits down and stands up a few times.)* Hoowah! Hoowah! Hoowah!

BERNARD: Stop it.

RORY: Kay.

(Beat)

BERNARD: Kid?

RORY: Yeah?

BERNARD: I feel like things would be easier for you if you toned it down a bit.

RORY: Toned what down?

BERNARD: Just your whole...

RORY: My whole...

BERNARD: Well, you're a little...

RORY: I'm a little...

(Beat)

BERNARD: Too much.

RORY: "Too much?" Ugh! Why does everyone say that to me? Too much of what?

BERNARD: Uhh...

RORY: What are you saying, you don't like me? Babies like me. Pearl laughs her head off whenever I'm around her. I'm gonna have a baby when I'm sixteen like on Teen Mom Two.

BERNARD: Terrible idea. Keep it in your pants til you get married, kid.

RORY: Keep what in my pants?

BERNARD: Forget it.

RORY: Oh, do you mean my lady goblet?

(BERNARD spits out his drink.)

RORY: I didn't realize I could take my lady goblet out. I thought it was all sorta tucked in there.

BERNARD: Um. It is…tucked in there. Who the hell told you to call it a lady goblet? Forget it, we need to end this conversation immediately.

RORY: But this is the only conversation I want to have!

BERNARD: "Give it a google." Isn't that what you kids say?

RORY: Can't. Lost my computer privileges this week due to my "sassy mouth". So yeah, yesterday I discovered I have more than just a peehole down there. Did you know that, Bernard? Did you know that I have more than just a peehole?

BERNARD: Yes, I did know that.

RORY: Well I wish you would've told ME! Talk about misinformed! So, I told my mom about my discovery and she said it was my lady goblet and that we shouldn't talk about it again until I'm married.

BERNARD: Your mom's a moron.

RORY: My dad calls her that too!

BERNARD: He does? That's awful.

RORY: Well he used to. He doesn't call her anything anymore 'cause they don't talk at all anymore.

BERNARD: Does he talk to you?

RORY: Yup! On Tuesdays. But he was busy the last six.

(Silence)

BERNARD: Your sister. Pearl, right?

RORY: Yeah?

BERNARD: She…got out via "lady goblet."

RORY: Huh?

BERNARD: Pearl exited your mother through her lady goblet.

RORY: THAT'S WHAT IT'S FOR??!

BERNARD: Among other things, yes. Don't they teach you anything in health class?

RORY: Well Sister Marylou runs health class and—

BERNARD: 'Nuff said.

RORY: My mind is blown! My young mind is blown!

BERNARD: Alright, simmer down, kid. Bernard is in desperate need of a new topic.

RORY: Okay, but I'm gonna circle back on this.

BERNARD: I'm sure you will.

RORY: So what are your summer vacation plans?

BERNARD: Staying local this year.

RORY: Every year I go to my Uncle Peter's pond. And you know what we do there? We skinny dip. That means swimming with no clothes on. You'd love it.

BERNARD: No I would not.

RORY: Well you can wear a bathing suit it you want to. But no goggles. That would be weird.

BERNARD: You've seen your extended family in a state of undress?

RORY: Totally. Nudity is sort of their thing. The only time I get uncomfortable is when the boys bounce on the diving board. *(Beat)* Oh man.

BERNARD: What.

RORY: I guess I'm not going this summer.

BERNARD: Why not?

RORY: Uncle Peter is my dad's brother. I guess I'm not invited since my dad broke up with my mom and me.

(Beat)

BERNARD: Dads don't break up with their daughters.

RORY: Mine did.

(Silence)

BERNARD: You wanted to see a picture of Chrissy?

RORY: Totally!

(BERNARD *pulls out his wallet.)*

RORY: What's that?

BERNARD: My wallet.

RORY: With paper pictures? How'd you think of that?

BERNARD: I'm a genius. Can you see okay from there?

RORY: Yup, my peepers are twenty twenty.

BERNARD: Alright, here she is when she was around your sister's age.

RORY: Aw, so cute!

BERNARD: Here's her first birthday party...

RORY: Wow, she's a ginger! Ya know, ginger people are supposed to have magical powers.

BERNARD: That so? I used to be a...a "ginger" as well.

RORY: No way! Why'd you stop?

BERNARD: Because my hair turned gray?

RORY: Gotcha. Oooh what's that one?

BERNARD: This here was her first ballet recital. Must've been about four?

RORY: Ballet is boring. She should've tapped.

BERNARD: She did actually. She did both. And here she was at her— She was uh— She was five and three quarters here.

RORY: How come her eyes are closed in that one?

BERNARD: She was sleeping.

RORY: In a box? Why was she all dressed up and sleeping in a box?

(Beat)

BERNARD: You want to see a picture of Irma?

RORY: Sure! Why was she mad at you before? Did you have a sleepover and not invite her?

BERNARD: No.

RORY: 'Cause my dad had a sleepover with the check-out lady from Shop Rite and didn't invite my mom. That got her real upset. I couldn't believe he did that, ya know? 'Cause like Whole Foods is so much better.

(Beat)

BERNARD: Here she is when we first met.

RORY: She's pretty! But why's she wearing that ugly green outfit?

BERNARD: We met while I was in the service.

RORY: You were a waitress?

BERNARD: A helicopter pilot.

RORY: Cool! Do you still fly?

BERNARD: No. I will never fly again as long as I live.

RORY: Me neither. I was on a plane to Disney world once and there was flatulence—

BERNARD: Turbulence.

RORY: Turbulence! And it made so many people sick. There were throwing up sounds and smells everywhere. Mickey wasn't worth it.

BERNARD: Irma was a photojournalist that came to our camp. She had to wear what we wore so she'd blend in.

RORY: But we were born to shine, Nard!

BERNARD: You did not want to shine over there, kid. Believe me, you wanted to blend.

(RORY *is suddenly distracted, watching something happening on her lawn.*)

RORY: Was Irma your first kiss?

BERNARD: First one that mattered. Only one since.

RORY: I haven't had my first kiss yet.

BERNARD: I should hope not. You're nine.

RORY: And a half! I practice on my bedpost. It has these bumps on it that look like lips. I also fold and squeeze my arm like this, but that looks a little like a butt too, and I'm not interested in putting my lips on any butts.

BERNARD: Yes, keep your lips…off butts.

RORY: You know who I really wish I could kiss? "Mohawk Paolo." That's what I call him.

BERNARD: That man has a moustache.

RORY: Right? He's nineteen.

BERNARD: Kid, have you ever heard the word "statutory"?

RORY: No.

BERNARD: …It's when a person is way too old to be kissing another person. And it's illegal.

RORY: Bob is ten years older than my mom. Is he statutory-ing her?

BERNARD: How old is your mother?

RORY: Thirty-seven.

BERNARD: I think she'll be fine. You, however…

RORY: Hold on Nard. (*Shouting to ground level*) Paolo! Paolo! Finito? Wait! I wanna tell you something importante. (*Beat*) Me gusta tu pelo. En mi opinion… mohawks? Son Buenos.

(RORY *gives* BERNARD *one more thumbs up, then collapses, giggling uncontrollably.*)

RORY: His mohawk really is mooey mooey bueno.

BERNARD: Get it together, kid.

RORY: You'd look cute with a mohawk, Nard. Congratulations on even having hair!

BERNARD: Thank you.

RORY: I thought all boys your age went bald. Does your hair feel loose? Tug it.

BERNARD: No.

RORY: Sometimes my ponytail pain gets so bad I wish I were bald. You probably don't know this, but if you wear a high pony for too long you get a super sore spot. I have one right now. If we were on the same roof would you rub it for me?

BERNARD: No. I would not rub any part of you.

RORY: Why not?

BERNARD: I value my freedom.

RORY: You're weird.

BERNARD: As are you.

(Beat)

RORY: Hey, I have an idea!!! Lift up your hand and scratch the air like you would if you were scratching my head. *(She pulls her ponytail out and dangles her hair forward.)*

BERNARD: What?

RORY: I'm a big senser of energy. I'll feel the rub without you even touching me. Lift and scratch Bernard!

BERNARD: No.

RORY: Please? I have pony pain! Lift and scratch!

BERNARD: No.

RORY: LIFT AND SCRATCH!

BERNARD: Ugh!

(BERNARD *lifts his hand and scratches in her direction.* RORY *shakes her head around happily.*)

RORY: Ugga-ugga-ugga-ugga-ugga-ugga. See? I can feel it! Keep going!

BERNARD: What am I—?

RORY: Keep going!

(BERNARD *keeps "scratching".* RORY*'s head keeps shaking.*)

RORY: Ugga-ugga-ugga-ugga-ugga-ugga. My hair skin is so happy right now you have no idea!

BERNARD: Alright, enough. *(He stops.)*

RORY: You stopped.

BERNARD: We're done.

RORY: But—

BERNARD: Done.

RORY: Alright. "I'll do it my damnself." *(She massages her own head for real.)* That's what my mom always says about things. "You can't be bothered to do the dishes, Bob? Fine. I'll do it my damnself." "You can't get your ass off the sofa to change a goddamn diaper? Fine. I'll do it my damnself." "I'm losing my mind here! You can't watch the baby for TWO hours so I can get a moment of peace? Fine, I'll do it my-"

BERNARD: Got the picture kid.

(RORY *stops rubbing her head. Beat*)

RORY: She cries a lot now.

BERNARD: Your mom?

RORY: Yeah.

BERNARD: Huh.

(Silence)

RORY: Can I come over? Like to your house?

BERNARD: Why?

RORY: So we can hang out.

BERNARD: We're "hanging out" now, aren't we?

RORY: No but like, I want to walk across your lawn, ring the doorbell, then get let inside and hang out with you in there.

BERNARD: No.

RORY: Why?

BERNARD: Because this...this is just fine.

RORY: But like what if I wanna high five you or pat you on the butt and say, "nice work, kid"?

BERNARD: No need for any of that.

RORY: But what if I want to?

BERNARD: Sorry.

(Beat)

RORY: Ya know what? Don't sweat it. Our houses are pretty close together, I bet I can leap to you.

BERNARD: Don't even think about it.

RORY: I'm a dancer. My leaps are amazing.

BERNARD: Leap when you're in the dance studio. When you're on the roof, you sit your ass back down.

RORY: Leap and the net will appear. Isn't that what people say?

BERNARD: That is what jackasses say.

RORY: Let's see... *(She walks to the edge of her roof.)*

RORY: Oh I can TOTALLY make this. Just need a running start.

BERNARD: Too close kid! Back up!

RORY: You're right. *(She scoots to the opposite side of her roof.)*

RORY: *(Singing)* I'm a big fine woman, gonna back my ass up. *(She runs at full speed across her roof.)*

BERNARD: NOOOOOOOOOOO!

RORY: Yay! UPS is here!!! *(She has stopped right at the edge of her roof.)*

BERNARD: Jesus Christ, Jesus H Christ.

RORY: My Legos are here, dude!

(BERNARD is on his knees, panting.)

BERNARD: Fanfuckintastic.

RORY: Nard, you okay?

BERNARD: *(Trying to recover)* Don't you ever do that again, you hear me?

RORY: I totally would've made it though!

BERNARD: I don't care.

RORY: But—

BERNARD: NEVER AGAIN!!!

RORY: Okay. *(Silence)* Does this mean you would you have been sad if I got hurt?

BERNARD: Of course I would.

RORY: Really? I didn't think you liked me.

(Beat)

BERNARD: Well, I do.

RORY: I LIKE YOU TOO NARD! SOOOO MUCH!!!!

BERNARD: Alright kid, don't burst a blood vessel.

RORY: I wish I could hug you right now! Wanna do an air hug? *(She opens her arms.)*

BERNARD: No thank you.

RORY: I think you could really use one though. Four actually. Did you know that people need four hugs a day?

BERNARD: That's an excessive amount of hugging.

RORY: And that's just for survival! It's four hugs for survival, eight for maintenance, and twelve for growth. If I got hugged more, maybe I wouldn't be so short.

(Beat)

BERNARD: Don't you get hugged?

RORY: From time to time.

(Beat)

(The faint sound of sirens. She puts her arms down.)

RORY: Wait. Do you hear that?

(They get a bit louder.)

RORY: Sirens. Ohmygod, sirens!

BERNARD: So?

RORY: They're getting closer! Ahhhh!

BERNARD: Easy, kid easy.

RORY: IT'S THE CONSUMER! THE CONSUMER FOUND US, NARD! WE'RE GOING TO THE SLAMMER!!

BERNARD: Shhh shhh shhh. I was pulling your leg about that. This is America. No one gives a shit what you do with your pellows.

RORY: Pillows.

BERNARD: Whatever. Some idiot ran the red-light on Cheltenham, that's all. Happens all time.

(The sirens get extremely loud and close. Beat)

RORY: So why are they in your driveway?

(The lights from the police cars swirl on both their faces.)

Part Three

(BERNARD is cleaning the leaves out of his gutters, his back to RORY's house. The cooler sits near him. He stops and takes a gulp of his drink.)

BERNARD: I know you're watching me. *(Beat)* I'm not a man oblivious to his surroundings. *(Beat)* You know, when you approach a person, it's customary to make your presence known. *(Beat)* Alright that's enough, stop staring at me.

RORY: I'm not staring at you! I'm gazing with wonder at the majesty of the falling leaves! *(She's popped her head out of her window.)*

BERNARD: Sure you are. *(He goes back to cleaning his gutters.)*

(Silence)

(RORY watches BERNARD.)

RORY: *(Whisper-yelling)* How are you? You've been hiding in your house so much lately.

BERNARD: Why are you whispering?

RORY: *(Whisper-yelling)* I'm not supposed to be talking to you.

BERNARD: Speak up, I can't hear you.

RORY: *(Whisper-yelling)* Everyone thinks you're dangerous and possibly disturbed.

BERNARD: *(Whisper-yelling back at her)* Ya know what? Perhaps whispering to a seventy-five year old man from a great distance isn't the best game plan for being heard.

RORY: What?

BERNARD: SPEAK UP!

RORY: EVERYONE THINKS YOU'RE A PSYCHO!

(Beat)

BERNARD: Well "everyone" is wrong. You know what a rumor is, kid?

RORY: Yes, it's the bump you get when you have cancer.

BERNARD: No…that's a tumor.

RORY: Right. Duh. *(Beat)* Well I'd better go downstairs and—

BERNARD: Look.

RORY: What?

BERNARD: *(Pointing)* Mousetraps. Took 'em down. All sparrows have been spared.

RORY: Oh. Good. *(Beat)* You're still killing people though, right?

BERNARD: What?! What is going on with you?

RORY: Sorry! The nervousness is making me say dumb things!

BERNARD: You're nervous talking to me?

RORY: Maybe!

BERNARD: Well that's ridiculous. I'm the same old Nard as before. Got any questions…just ask me.

RORY: Okay. *(Beat)* Why were the police at your house that day? Were you caught murdering or loitering or something? Why do you drink Jim Beam juice all the time when there are so many other flavors in the world? Do you think I'm pretty? Do you like having weeds in your yard or are you too lazy to give them a good mowing? Would you consider yourself a sad person or a happy person? Do you think I'm smart?

Do you get scared when you go to confession too?
Why don't you ever drive a car? How come you lied
about having a daughter? How come I've never met
your wife? Are you hiding them? Or did you do like
something very bad to them? Oh and, I've missed you.
Have you missed me?

(Beat)

BERNARD: If I was caught murdering or loitering,
would I be out here "gazing in wonder at the majesty
of the falling leaves"?

RORY: Ha! Probably not.

BERNARD: Definitely not. I would be in prison.

RORY: Wearing a cool orange jumpsuit!

BERNARD: I suppose so, yes.

RORY: I think your silvery hair would look real nice
against the orange.

BERNARD: Regardless… *(Beat)* I drink Jim Beam juice
because I like it, I don't drive a car because I don't need
to, and the police were at my house that day because
Irma called them.

RORY: Why'd she call 'em?

BERNARD: She was scared.

RORY: Of what?

BERNARD: She couldn't find Chrissy.

(Beat)

*(RORY leaps out onto her roof. She's wearing her school
uniform and has a Starbucks cup in hand.)*

RORY: Ohmygosh I forgot! I have some news that's
gonna rock your world! Are you ready?

(Beat)

(BERNARD *downs his drink and pours another. He goes back to cleaning the gutters.*)

RORY: Nard.
Nard.
Nard.
Nard.
Nard.
Nard.
Nard.

BERNARD: What?

RORY: Are you ready?

BERNARD: Fine. Yes.

RORY: I WAS CAST IN THE FALL MUSICAL!!!!

BERNARD: Alright.

RORY: We're doing Grease! And I'm Rizzo!

BERNARD: At a Catholic school?

RORY: Well, we crossed out a lot of words in our scripts. "Summer Lovin" got changed to "Seasonal Hand-holding", "Lousy with virginity" became "empowered by her vocation", and instead of referring to Grease Lightnin' as a "pussy wagon", we're now calling it a "kitten parade float". *(Beat)* Oh and in our version, Rizzo's not afraid she's pregnant, she's concerned she may have caught Kenickie's cough.

BERNARD: High drama, huh?

RORY: Totally.

BERNARD: Well, congrats kid. Good for you.

RORY: Thanks. Our first rehearsal was yesterday. Mrs. Conaway, the speech teacher spent the whole first hour yelling at the girls for using vocal fry. Will you come see it?

BERNARD: Uh…

RORY: I plan on being really good.

BERNARD: I'm just not—

RORY: It's okay, you don't have to. I know you never leave the house.

(Beat)

BERNARD: I leave the house.

RORY: Oh yeah?

BERNARD: Yeah.

RORY: Like when?

BERNARD: Like…right now.

RORY: Doesn't count if you're standing ON the house.

BERNARD: You're right. I guess it doesn't. *(He smiles.)*

RORY: You're pretty when you smile, Nard.

(Beat)

BERNARD: Thanks kid.

(BERNARD *reaches for his drink.* RORY *lifts her Starbucks cup.)*

RORY: Bottom's up, friend!

(BERNARD *and* RORY *drink.)*

BERNARD: Whatcha drinkin' there, sport?

RORY: Pumpkin Spice latte.

BERNARD: Oh, Christ, you're one of them?

RORY: Absolutely. Bob and I get one every day after school when he picks me up.

BERNARD: Decaf I hope.

RORY: No, we like it "high octane, baby."

(Beat)

BERNARD: Been having some quality time with your "bonus dad," huh?

RORY: Sort of. My mom's away for a while, so.

BERNARD: Yeah? Where'd she go?

RORY: To a spa.

BERNARD: Lucky her.

RORY: Not really. She has The Partum.

(Beat)

BERNARD: The—postpartum de—

RORY: Yeah. That. So Bob sent her to a spa.

BERNARD: Where's your sister?

RORY: Staying with Bob's Mom, Nonna Theresa. Hey, I went on a hayride today for a class trip.

(Beat)

BERNARD: You have a good time?

RORY: Sorta. But like when are they gonna invent a hayride that doesn't itch your butt, ya know? Anyway I got you something. I was gonna put it on your stoop then ring the doorbell and run away, but since you're here...hold on.

(RORY climbs inside her window. BERNARD finishes his drink and refills.)

RORY: *(Yelling from inside the house)* Don't look, okay? I want it to be a surprise! Close your eyes!

BERNARD: Okay.

RORY: Are they closed?!

BERNARD: Yup.

RORY: No they're not! I can tell by the way you said "yup"!

(BERNARD finishes refilling his glass.)

BERNARD: Okay, hang on...hold on...okay, now they're closed.

RORY: Okay! *(She hops back out on the roof carrying two pumpkins.)* Aaaaaaaand…open.

(BERNARD does. She holds one pumpkin over her head.)

RORY: "It's decorative gourd season, motherfuckers!"

(RORY throws the pumpkin at BERNARD.)

BERNARD: Holy shit!

RORY: Nice catch, friend. Sorry for saying "motherfuckers". Bob had a "cocktail party" with his pals the other night and his one loud friend kept saying "It's decorative gourd season, motherfuckers!" Oh shoot I said it again. Twice.

BERNARD: It's okay. *(He pokes at his pumpkin's "face".)* Why is it—

RORY: Oh, they're pre-carved!

BERNARD: What?

RORY: That way we can "Keep the 'Boo' while avoiding the 'boo-boos' this Halloween." Get it?

BERNARD: Childhood today is a sanitized shit show.

RORY: Huh?

(Beat)

BERNARD: Thanks, kid. Very sweet of you.

RORY: You're welcome! Wanna scoop the guts out with me? There's a recyclable spoon inside, as well as a biodegradable baggy and an electric candle. We just gut him, poke his eyes and teeth out, then light him on battery-operated fire.

BERNARD: Alright, let's do it.

RORY: YEAH???

BERNARD: YEAH!!

RORY: Sweet.

(RORY *starts scooping her pumpkin with gusto.* BERNARD *slowly gets into it.)*

(Silence for a bit as they work.)

RORY: The other day when I was inside Harriet Tubman, I had this really wild thought about you.

BERNARD: Whoa…when you were inside whom?

RORY: Harriet Tubman. My bathtub. That's cool how you use "whom" properly.

BERNARD: You named your bathtub?

RORY: I name everything. I'm an anthropomorphosist.

BERNARD: Alright.

RORY: So I was inside Harriet and I realized that you and I are only overlapping for a little bit.

BERNARD: What do you mean?

RORY: Like on the planet. I was kinda just born and pretty soon you're gonna die.

BERNARD: Okay…

RORY: Like, I don't have much past and you don't have much future.

BERNARD: Wow…

RORY: So that makes this little bit of overlappy time we have together super special. We gotta give it all we got. *(Beat)* Hey Nard, check it. *(She "sneezes" out some pumpkin guts.)* Ah-choooo!

BERNARD: That's gross, kid.

RORY: I know, right?! You try.

(Beat)

(BERNARD *"throws up" some pumpkin guts. He makes throwing up sound.)*

RORY: NICE NARD! My turn. *(Throwing up sound)* Your turn!

(BERNARD *makes grotesquely exaggerated throwing up sounds.)*

RORY: This is amazing!! Hey, I bet if we really focus, we could create a pumpkin snot rocket. Here, put some guts up to your nose and—

BERNARD: Yeah, I think that's where I draw my line, kid.

RORY: Kay.

(Silence)

(BERNARD *and* RORY *go back to scooping. He drinks more.)*

RORY: Could you ask me "How was school today, honey?"?

(Beat)

BERNARD: "How was school today...honey?"

RORY: Really interesting, thanks. Mark McGuire accidentally ate his Nana's medical marijuana muffin and had to go to the hospital. He said his whole body was vibrating up and down. "How was YOUR day, honey?"

BERNARD: My day?

RORY: Yeah.

BERNARD: Pretty...mixed.

RORY: What'd you do?

BERNARD: I took the bus to visit Irma at her new place.

RORY: Why's Irma have a new place? Isn't she supposed to live with you in your place?

BERNARD: Yes she is. But she's sick. I had to move her someplace where doctors could take care of her.

RORY: What's wrong with her?

BERNARD: Well…sometimes she doesn't know who I am.

RORY: You think she has The Partum?

BERNARD: No she doesn't.

RORY: 'Cause my mom's like that too. She's always like "Bob, I don't know who you ARE anymore!"

BERNARD: No, that's different. Irma doesn't know where she is or what she's doing a lot of the time.

RORY: Same thing with mom! She's like "Bob, I need some time to FIND myself!"

BERNARD: No no, that's—

RORY: I don't know what she's talking about though. She's super easy to find! She's always standing at the kitchen sink staring out the window. "Women!," huh?

BERNARD: CAN I TALK, KID?!?

(Beat)

RORY: Sure. Yeah.

BERNARD: Sorry, I don't mean to yell I'm just…

RORY: It's okay. *(Beat)* Go on.

BERNARD: Okay. *(Beat. He drinks.)* She gets confused. Imagines things are the way they used to be. I always know we're in trouble when she wakes up to the sounds of those goddamn birds outside the window. She loves the sound those little fuckers make. 'Scuse me. They're not "fuckers". They're just—it puts her in this headspace that… *(Beat)* On those mornings, she leans over and kisses me real softly. I pretend to still be asleep. I love that kiss, even though I know what it means. Then I listen to her tiptoe down the hall so she doesn't wake us. She starts scrambling eggs in the kitchen. Makes a peanut butter and jelly sandwich and puts it in a Ziploc bag. I know what she's doing.

I know why she's doing it. And I let her, even though I know what's coming next. I know the consequences, but I don't try to stop it. I actually try to stretch those moments out for her as long as possible, because her face is softer. Her voice is lighter. Even her footsteps sound happy when she's in that world. *(Beat)* Then little things start tripping her up. "Why isn't Chrissy's uniform on the hook? I put her uniform on the hook." "Honey, have you seen Chrissy's lunchbox?" I can explain some things away, but eventually the panic reaches her face. When she starts searching the rooms for her, I have to tell her. I have to tell her again, like it's the first time she's hearing it. And I have to watch her remember. *(Beat)* Watching her remember is a thousand times worse than seeing her forget. *(Silence. He drinks.)*

RORY: Have you thought about—

BERNARD: I used to run my finger along her gums as much as she'd let me. Tried to memorize the feel of it. "She loves to gnaw on my fingers", I'd say. But she didn't. Not really. She was accommodating me. Every time she'd cut a new tooth, I got this pit in my stomach. She was changing so quickly. Felt like I couldn't keep up. I wanted to keep her small. I'd say "You're growing up too fast, kid. Slow down for Daddy, will ya?" There's not a more ridiculous thing you can say to a child. Not a more selfish thing. Stop growing? Fucking moron. It's a damn privilege to watch a child growing up. I'd give anything to have seen six, ten, sixteen, twenty-one, thirty. I just—I can't imagine how different my life would be if there were a forty-year-old woman standing in front of me right now.

(Beat)

RORY: My Aunt Judy is forty. It's not that exciting when she stands in front of me, but I could ask her to do it for you if you like.

BERNARD: Chrissy. My daughter, Chrissy. She'd be forty now if she'd...

RORY: Oh. Okay that makes sense. *(Beat)* I'm really sorry Nard.

(Silence)

(BERNARD finishes his drink and pours another full glass.)

RORY: Have you thought about talking to a lady once a week?

BERNARD: Sorry?

RORY: I talk to a lady once a week now. She says things like "you deserve love" and "it's okay to cry." Her office smells like tuna, but she's pretty nice.

BERNARD: Yeah... That's never gonna happen.

RORY: Okay. *(Beat)* You gonna see Irma again soon?

BERNARD: In a couple days, yeah.

RORY: Cool. I have something that might make her feel better. Gimme a sec.

(RORY dashes into her house. BERNARD drinks.)

(RORY pops out holding a lifelike doll.)

RORY: Go long Nard!

(RORY hurls the doll in BERNARD's direction. It socks him directly in the chest.)

BERNARD: Christ!

RORY: Sorry. You okay?

BERNARD: ...Yeah. *(He holds the doll by her foot and inspects it.)*

RORY: She's for Irma, since she misses Chrissy so much. I think she might like holding her.

BERNARD: Oh, I don't think—well that's very... But don't you need her?

RORY: Duh! I'm in fifth grade now. All I need is iTunes and slime.

BERNARD: Alright.

RORY: She's in great shape. Just don't flip her over, she has crayon stains all over her butt. I scrubbed 'em off her face, but her butt stuff just won't budge. Her name is Netflix.

BERNARD: Why Netflix?

RORY: 'Cause my brother's a psycho and convinced me that's what all the girls were naming their dolls when I was three.

BERNARD: Whoa... Since when do you have a brother?

RORY: He's in Sin-sin-atty with my dad. Yeah, it was boys against girls when we moved.

(BERNARD *stumbles*.)

RORY: Whoa, Nard, whoa!

BERNARD: I'm alright.

RORY: You're alright?

BERNARD: Yeah, I'm alright.

RORY: Kay.

(BERNARD *knocks back the rest of his drink and moves toward his window.*)

BERNARD: Alright kid, I'm gonna call it a— (*He stumbles again.*)

RORY: Nard! Do me a solid and sit down, K?

BERNARD: "Do you a—"

RORY: A solid. Cool people say "do me a solid."

BERNARD: *(Laughing)*Do you a solid…

RORY: It means "be a pal and do me a favor, huh?" Can you do me a favor and sit down?

(BERNARD stumbles again, this time quite close to the edge.)

RORY: NARD! SIT DOWN DUDE!

BERNARD: Yeah, you're right kid. You're right. *(He sits.)*

RORY: There you go.

(BERNARD cradles the doll.)

(He starts rocking it.)

(Silence)

RORY: You think Irma will like her? *(Beat)* She can call her whatever she wants. Chrissy, Netflix, Ruh-JAI-nuh…whatever she wants.

(BERNARD holds the doll tight to his chest and starts to cry.)

RORY: Are you…? *(Beat)* Gosh, um.

(BERNARD continues to cry.)

(RORY watches him.)

RORY: Shhhhhh. It's okay. Shhhhh.

(After a few moments, BERNARD quiets.)

(Silence)

RORY: Getting dark, huh? *(Beat)* Yeah. Getting dark. *(Beat)* Have you named your pumpkin yet? *(Beat)* I think my mine's name is Gourd-on Lightfoot. Get it? GOURD-on? *(Beat)* Should we light them? See how they look? *(Beat)* Alright, I'll go first. *(She places the electric candle in her pumpkin and turns it on. It glows.)* Look, he's smiling at you.

(BERNARD just stares off.)

RORY: It's okay, Nard. It's gonna be okay.

Part Four

(There are patches of snow and ice on the roofs.)

*(*Rory *is in her window, tossing tiny red objects at* Bernard's *house. After many misses and a few good hits, his window finally opens and he appears. He looks down at his roof, littered with red.)*

Bernard: Swedish fish, huh?

Rory: Yeah. I tried Cheerios for about a half hour, but they were not effective. *(Beat)* Hi.

Bernard: Hi. *(Beat)* Shouldn't you be in school?

Rory: *(Cough, cough)* I'm sick.

Bernard: Oh yeah??

Rory: *(Sneeze! Cough! Disgusting slurpy nose-blowing sound!)* Yeah.

Bernard: 'Cause it sounds like you're milkin' it, a little bit there, Bessie.

Rory: Nope. I'm for real sick.

Bernard: Okay. Someone over there taking care of you?

Rory: Yeah, my mom's back. But whatever, I'm ten now, I can take care of myself.

Bernard: Wait, I thought you were nine.

Rory: Had a birthday last week.

Bernard: Oh. How was it?

Rory: Eh. Just a day.

(Beat)

Bernard: Just a day?

Rory: Yeah. *(Beat)* Sometimes I feel like extra in my family.

BERNARD: Extra? Extra what?

RORY: I dunno, just…extra.

(Beat)

BERNARD: Happy birthday, kid.

RORY: Thanks. *(Beat)* I can see your breath.

BERNARD: Pretty cold, yeah.

RORY: I bet it smells.

BERNARD: My breath?

RORY: Yeah, you seem like someone who would have smelly breath.

(Beat)

BERNARD: I see yours too, you know.

RORY: Yeah, but mine is so minty it's crazy. I brush after every meal.

BERNARD: Good for you. You keep that up.

RORY: I will. *(Beat)* Fuck flossing though, yeah? *(She starts to cry.)*

BERNARD: Whoa, whoa, hey.

RORY: Fuck, I shouldn't say fuck! Fuck, I shouldn't say fuck!

BERNARD: What's going on, kid?

RORY: I saw your stupid sign.

(Beat)

BERNARD: Oh.

RORY: Why didn't you tell me you were moving?

BERNARD: I was going to, but…

RORY: Where are you going?

BERNARD: Just a couple towns over so I can be closer to Irma.

RORY: But she doesn't even know who you are!

BERNARD: Yeah, but I know who she is.

(*Silence*)

RORY: What about me?

BERNARD: You'll be fine, kid. (*Beat*) I was thinking…I could give you my new address if you want.

RORY: Why would I want that?

BERNARD: I thought maybe you could draw me a picture or send me a letter from time to time.

(*Beat*)

RORY: Maybe.

(*Silence*)

BERNARD: You were a real good Rizzo.

RORY: You came???

BERNARD: I did.

RORY: Ohmygosh, did you like it???

BERNARD: Not one bit.

RORY: Oh.

(*Beat*)

BERNARD: The show was terrible, but you… you lit up the room, kid.

RORY: Oh. (*Beat*) Thanks. (*Silence*) Did Irma like Netflix?

BERNARD: She did. Very much.

RORY: She didn't mind her butt stains?

BERNARD: Didn't seem to, no.

RORY: That's good.

(*Silence*)

BERNARD: Can you put some shoes?

RORY: I guess. Why?

BERNARD: Just put them on. You got a sweater or something nearby?

RORY: Yeah.

BERNARD: Put that on too.

RORY: Why, what are we—

BERNARD: Just "do me a solid" and do it, okay?

RORY: Ha! Okay. *(She disappears from view for a moment. She reappears, zipping up her hoodie and wiggling into her shoes.)* Okay. Now what?

BERNARD: We're gonna climb on out, nice and easy.

RORY: But it's wintertime.

BERNARD: This'll only take a second.

(Beat)

RORY: Wait. Have you had any juice today?

(Beat)

BERNARD: No I have not. I've been…discovering the joys of tea.

RORY: Ohmygosh you have to try Egyptian oolong when you get a chance!

BERNARD: I will do that. You ready?

RORY: Yeah.

climb out their windows.)

BERNARD: Be real careful. Look out for icy spots.

RORY: Kay.

(BERNARD and RORY stand across from one another.)

RORY: What are we doing?

(Beat)

BERNARD: I'm gonna miss you, kid.

(Beat)

(For once, RORY *is speechless.* BERNARD *opens his arms.)*

RORY: *(Gasp)* An air hug?

BERNARD: An air hug.

RORY: I can't believe it!

BERNARD: Well, believe it.

RORY: This is so unlike you though!

BERNARD: Yeah, well.

RORY: I just can't believe you're going to give me—

BERNARD: *(With his arms still out)* You want the hug or not.

(Beat)

RORY: So much. *(She opens her arms.)*

*(*BERNARD *and* RORY *walk into a "hug", their arms curled around the air in the shape of each other's bodies.)*

*(*RORY *tilts her head as though it rests on his chest.)*

(Silence)

BERNARD: Rory?

RORY: Yeah?

BERNARD: You're not extra. *(Beat)* No way are you extra, kid.

*(*BERNARD *and* RORY *stay in their positions, hugging each other's air.)*

*(*RORY *closes her eyes and smiles.)*

END OF PLAY